No More Pity Parties

A Guide to Celebrating Your Way Through Life

by

June Hall

McGREGOR
PUBLISHING

Library of Congress Cataloging-in-Publication Data
Hall, June, 1965–
    No more pity parties : a guide to celebrating
       your way through life / June Hall
     p. cm.
    Includes bibliographical references.
    ISBN 0-9653846-4-0 (alk. paper)
    1. Conduct of life. 2. Interpersonal relations. I. Title.

BF637.C5 .H294 2000
158—dc21

                   99-045952

Interior design and typesetting by Sue Knopf, Graffolio.

Poem, "my reflection," which appears on page 24, used with permission by giovanni singleton.

Cartoons used with permission by Jeffrey Gresham.

Published by McGregor Publishing, Inc., Tampa, Florida.

Printed and bound in the United States of America.

To the love of my life, Tim, my husband,
best friend, confidant, counselor
and soulmate;
and to the greatest mother ever (mine!)
for keeping the candle lit
to help me find my way.

Contents

Introduction

$\mathcal{L}$ ife is a continuous combination of varied experiences—the good, the not-so-good, the extremely painful, the swift, the brief, the lingering and even those that repeat themselves. Although we cannot always control life's experiences, we can control our responses to them. Taking control of our responses changes us from being swept along by these experiences to managing our lives.

When we are being swept along, we feel powerless. The experience is in complete control. This often creates more problems, as we may end up in even more stressful situations. Even if, by chance, the experience deposits us in a safe landing, we do not know how we got there. Consequently, we have not learned from it. We do not know how to effect the same outcome again, nor how to apply what occurred to other situations.

Managing our lives during our experience is a purposeful action. We assess the situation and our own strength and determine our strategy to achieve the desired outcome. We are working toward a goal instead of just accepting whatever we get. Even when the experience is painful, deciding how we are going to work through the pain, instead of just drowning in it, helps us retain our power.

This book focuses on helping people successfully navigate through life, regardless of their experiences. It does this by highlighting four themes: self-esteem, single life, relationships and life dilemmas. As long as you live, your life will be affected by these themes, either directly or indirectly. The more knowledge and skills you have for dealing with them, the less likely you are to be overwhelmed by your experiences.

Because these themes are generic to the human experience, this book is for everyone, not just those experiencing problems in a certain area. If you are coping well, the information here could enhance the quality of your life. The many techniques and approaches listed in these pages may provide insight on how you deal with issues and expand your repertoire of coping skills.

The author, June Hall, has spent her professional career working with people of all ages from diverse backgrounds with different needs and concerns. As an educator, she taught students who were at risk of dropping out of school. Her creativity and her ability to connect with and motivate students helped them improve their academic skills and their self-esteem. In her second year, she was nominated for Teacher of the Year at her school.

As a counselor, she helped individuals, couples and families cope with tough issues. From her experiences, she became aware that certain themes are threaded through the range of human problems. She began to conduct workshops and speak about these issues to numerous groups. Her passion and commitment captured her audiences, and she became a popular speaker, often requested by businesses and human services organizations.

In her desire to reach more people, June began writing an advice column four years ago. Her no-nonsense, cut-to-the-chase column is now published in newspapers in Fort Lauderdale and St. Petersburg in Florida, Boston, Mass., and Toledo, Ohio. The response to her column has been extremely positive, and she is currently working on syndication.

This book pulls together the wealth of experience, knowledge and practical wisdom that June's column readers have come to expect. It will be a valuable resource to anyone trying to manage the ups and downs of life...and aren't we all.

Dorothy Osgood, Ph.D., LSW
Associate Professor, Social Work
Shippensburg University
Shippensburg, PA

Pilot Your Own Plane

with Soaring Self-Esteem

The next time you look in the mirror,
repeat these words:
"I am the greatest me that will ever be."
And don't ever forget it!

My 2¢

$\mathcal{I}$ found out in my late teen years that being myself is one of my most important duties—but I had to learn it the hard way. Like most teen-agers, my self-esteem was tied to fitting in with my peers. It bothered me that I did not have that pretty-girl model look. I was everyone's friend, both boys and girls, but nobody's girlfriend. I didn't want just any boy, either; I wanted to be cute enough to have the pick of the litter. I had to have "Mr. Popular."

When I was 13, a schoolmate tried to walk with me after school to ask me to be his girlfriend, but I hurried away. He wasn't the type I had set my sights on. By the time I made it home, I felt terrible. I certainly wouldn't have wanted anyone to treat me so coldly. The next day, I tried to befriend him. Of course, he wanted nothing to do with me. That day I walked away from someone who is now a great husband and father, because I thought I needed a "Mr. Popular" to make me feel special. Fortunately, I learned that I needed to make myself feel special, instead of waiting for someone else to do it for me.

That encounter in junior high sparked a period of discovery for me. Over time I realized that the guys chose me as a friend—as opposed to a girlfriend—not because I was unattractive, but because, at that age, many of them were looking for something else in their dates. They were thrilled with flirtation and with the thought of physical intimacy. That is not what I wanted for myself, and I am thankful to my parents for the high standards they taught me. Also, I used my brain. Many of the "pretty girls" were so focused on their looks and attracting boys, they came off as airheads—though most of them were much smarter than they acted.

As it turned out, I'm glad I didn't take a walk on the "cool side." Tim and I got together, and today we have been married for six years.

Another lesson I have learned about self-esteem is that the more confidence people have in themselves, the more attractive they are. We all know people who don't have model-perfect faces and figures, but there is something engaging about them. It's the way they carry themselves and believe in themselves. On the other hand, sometimes those who look the best are covering up their own insecurities.

I once worked with a lady whose hair, makeup and clothes always looked great. I told her I envied the way she fixed herself so nicely. She said she envied me for not going through all the trouble, because she had to get up at least 30 minutes earlier every morning. I said I didn't understand why she would go through all that trouble. Her response was she didn't feel good enough about herself that she could leave the house without being made up, but she wished she had the confidence to do so.

At first, I was surprised by this information. I always thought people with low self-esteem were too depressed to care about their appearance. In some cases, this is true, but it works both ways. Sometimes you need the boost of dressing up for the world. I say, if it floats your boat, stay on board. Just make sure you realize that looks aren't everything. They eventually fade, but your confidence and personality can last a lifetime.

Low self-esteem shows itself in many ways. People exposed to abuse, for instance, are often so uncertain of themselves, they have to exert power over others to feel good. Others get so caught up in the role of victim, they can't get out of it. This cycle leads to a host of self-destructive behaviors, including family violence, crime, prostitution and substance abuse. People caught in this cycle need treatment. If you or anyone you love fits into this category, it is essential to get help. (See the resource list at the back of the book.)

Often people who don't feel good about themselves look to others to fix their problems. It's good to have supportive people around you, but the conviction has to come from within. It may sound strange, but when I had down periods in my life, some of my friends supported those negative feelings.

I did not realize this at the time. My mom has a saying that goes: "When you are in the hole, you can't really see in it; but once you get out of the hole, you can look down in the hole and really see what's in there." Once I stepped away, analyzed the situation and starting looking for the positive, I became a much better person. You know what else happened? I began projecting positive feelings, which attracted positive people.

This became crystal clear when I started my advice column four years ago. A friend laughed.

Someone else said, "Don't count on it." When it did happen, my brother was so proud he started telling friends and relatives. One of the relatives came to me and said, "Robert told me you started a column, but he didn't explain it right. He said it was like an advice column, like a Dear Abby. That's not right, is it?"

I told her that was exactly right. Her attitude just blew my mind. She was planting seeds of doubt. Could this really work? SLAP! Of course this could really work. I believed in myself enough to pursue it. That's support system No. 1: believing in yourself and turning a deaf ear to those who try to feed you negative information.

When facing a life decision, sometimes you just have to go with your gut instinct. Let's say you want to be a singer, but someone tells you that your voice is not strong enough, or that it's too tough to make it in the entertainment field. Realize that it's not what others think you should do, but what you believe in yourself that you CAN do. That's what having good self-esteem is all about. There are many singers out there with enormous talent, but they lack the self-confidence to show it off. On the other hand, there are artists with limited talent who are making a living with their music. They wanted it, they believed they could achieve it, and they went out there and did it. You should too.

7

It doesn't matter if you "make it" or not. What's important is that you go for it. My dad used to say, "Nothing beats a failure, but a try." Once you try, you've already succeeded.

Of course, a support system does make any effort easier. Sometimes, if friends and family are in a negative place, you have to create your own circle of positivity by cultivating supportive relationships. Look for people who are there for you — even if they disagree with some of your decisions. If your attempts don't turn out as well as you had hoped, these people won't say, "I told you so." When the chips are down, they will help pick them up. If no one immediately comes to mind, look for groups where you will find others who share your values, at a church, temple, school or professional organization, for example. Your support system doesn't have to be a large number of people. I only have a handful, but they're the best handful of positive people anyone could have.

Sure, you may still hear negative comments. You can't control what others say, only your reaction to it. If you build strength from the inside out, you can withstand any storm.

I often get questions about self-esteem from my readers. Here are some memorable columns on the topic:

Related Advice

Dear June: How do you go about rebuilding self-esteem? —CT

Dear CT: When you say rebuilding, I presume that means you once had it. You must have let something or someone interfere with your self-esteem. The first step would be to remove yourself from the negative situation or person. If you cannot leave physically, you must detach emotionally. You can do this by turning to other interests: meditation, Bible study, a hobby group, etc. It also helps your mental state to get physically active—join an aerobics or karate class or take dance lessons.

Flood your brain with positive thoughts. Yes, I want you to talk to yourself. Every morning, look in the mirror and say something good to yourself, something different every day. I'm sure you can find at least seven wonderful comments about yourself each week. It may be hard at first, but after a while, you'll start believing all that good stuff—and believing in yourself.

So don't waste another second. Get started today.

● ● ●

Dear June: I am a student in psychology, and I was in an abusive relationship, married to a man who beat me. The only reason I stayed in that relationship is because I didn't have the support of friends and family to help me out of it. I had

9

no self-esteem, and it took me years of counseling to get over it.   —Beth

Dear Beth: You beat the odds! Many abused
women have good support systems, go through
therapy and still decide to stay with their abuser
or to go back to him. It's up to the victim to
stop being a victim and to say, just as you did, "I
don't want to live like this anymore." Seeking
help is the first step. Most communities have
hotlines to help those in crisis, or call 1-800-799-
SAFE for the shelter nearest you. (Note:
Although we hear more about women, men can
be the victims of abuse, and they, too need to
seek help.)

• • •

Dear June: The response you gave Black and
Tired moved me to tears. You said you know
black women who have no clue about their race
and try to "be down." Do you know how much
that statement hurts women like me, who are
trying to fit in and figure out where we belong?
I'm 24, and my family moved to a predominant-
ly white neighborhood when I was 10. I'm active
in the arts and politics and have traveled exten-
sively throughout the States and Europe. The
variance of races and cultures that exist are not
a mystery to me; yet I feel as though my own
race is unaccepting of me. I don't know what it
means to be black. I want to get the punch
lines! I've decided to transfer my studies to
Atlanta because I want to know what I've been
missing.

It's beliefs like yours—that there's a way to be black—that continue to cause rifts in our race.

— Lost in the Middle of the Party, Boca Raton, FL

Dear Lost: Your letter moved me as well. I am so sorry that you are going through this. Let me explain my thoughts: You are mistaken that I believe there is "a way" to be black. What I do believe and practice is that there is a way to be me. There is also a way to be you. Your challenge is not learning how to be black, it's accepting who and what you are.

Like you, I did not grow up in the 'hood; however, it seems I did have more exposure to my race, through family, friends and African-American events. Did I try to fit in? Sure, until I matured and realized that it was not healthy to change the way I was in order to gain acceptance. You should realize this, too.

The point I am trying to make is this: Do not try to "be down," be yourself! If you do not get the punch lines, you need new jokes. If friends and acquaintances make you feel uncomfortable, move on. It's OK to be different. It's also OK to learn more about your race. It's not OK to force yourself to drink milk when it does not agree with your system.

Do not try to force yourself to be what you clearly are not. If you keep this up, you will never be happy. Not every single person you meet will like you. Accept this and find people — regardless of race — who like you just the way you are. JUST BE YOURSELF!

The Heart of the Matter

*Y*es! Yes! You are beautiful, talented, smart, a good worker, caring, sophisticated, motivated, terrific, marvelous, swell . . . just an all-around great person.

Self-esteem is the positive belief in one's self. That's why I am beginning this section with positive adjectives. As the old saying goes: If you do not believe in yourself, who else will? So let's get to work.

We will look at three aspects of self-esteem:

1. How we allow it to get torn down
2. How we build it up
3. How we maintain it

LOSING SELF-ESTEEM

To understand self-esteem, we must look at the ways we let life circumstances undermine it. Sometimes we allow abuse, lack of praise or failure to erode our belief in ourselves. Especially when we are children, negative messages and situations can become ingrained in our psyches. As adults, however, we have the choice to continue to live out negative patterns or to break free of them. But we have to be willing to fight, not physically, but emotionally. This means tuning out the negative statements that play in our brains or that we hear from others. It means replacing them with positive affirmations and situations.

Let's say your mate frequently tells you that you're fat. You continually take in this message, and you start believing that you can never be shapely. Even if you are not actually overweight, you may allow yourself to overeat because you have internalized this message.

This is not to say that one must be a certain size to have positive self-worth. My sister, Lois, is full-figured, and most people call her beautiful and just adore her, myself included. Why? Because she does not let her weight get her down. She always dresses well, looks great and has personality plus. In other words, she has good self-esteem.

Another woman I know—we'll call her Mary— was not so fortunate. An attractive woman with a shapely figure and a cute face, Mary became involved with an average-looking man named John. The relationship was marvelous at first, then the subtle insults began:

"Mary, maybe you should wear your hair in a different style."

"Are you really wearing that to the party?"

"That skirt is a little tight, isn't it?"

"Maybe you should wear less makeup."

"I don't trust your best friend, and I don't want her in our house."

Mary, who is happy to have a man in her life, accepts what John says to please him. Why would she allow this? She entered into this relationship with low self-confidence; therefore, she empowers him so he won't leave her. Now that John has Mary in his corner without her support system, he can pretty much sell her on his ideas. There is no equity in the relationship. She changes her physical look as well as her outlook. She lets John choose her wardrobe. She finds herself having limited contact with her friends and family. She balloons from a size 9 to an 18, and her self-esteem plummets. Mary has nowhere to go but up, and we'll check in on her later to see what happens in her life.

We can sympathize with Mary because she wants what we all want—a good relationship. You must first have a good relationship with yourself, however, so that you won't let others tear down your self-confidence. If you understand yourself, and you like who you are, you will be able to establish healthy, give-and-take relationships with others.

It can happen the other way around, too: A lady can be hard on her man. He sends her flowers; she says they're the wrong kind. He gets a job promotion;

it's not enough money. He buys a new suit; it's the wrong cut. After a while, he feels he cannot please her, and he loses faith in himself. There goes his working toward promotions. And forget about further relationships—he cannot succeed at this one. Now he is in a rut because he has taken in all his mate's garbage.

He doesn't have to stay in that rut, however, and neither do you. There will always be people who seem intent on tearing down your self-confidence. Only you have the power to deflect negative messages. This is why it is so important to have what respected behavioral therapist Julian Rotters called internal locus of control. This means you generate your own feelings of self-worth, which you can control. Otherwise, your self-esteem will be based on outside forces (external locus of control), which you cannot control. The good news is that if you have been taking in negativity from the outside, you have the power to put yourself in charge.

REGAINING SELF-ESTEEM

So once you've let the world chip away at your self-esteem, how do you build it back? We will talk about three simple steps:

1. Remove yourself from the negative situation.

2. Live how you would like to see yourself live.
3. Feed yourself positive messages.

To rebuild your self-esteem you must distance yourself from a situation that is tearing you down. If you can't remove yourself physically, do so mentally by listening to motivational tapes and picturing the way you would like to see yourself live. Start each day by saying something positive about yourself, and make it your mantra for the day. By placing yourself mentally in a positive space and utilizing your internal locus of control, you can physically live or work in a negative environment and still improve your lifestyle.

Picture the life you want, write it down and keep it close to you. Your plan of action is to make your picture come to life. Exercise, go to church or temple, join a woodworking group—do whatever your plan calls for. Surround yourself with positive people and discover their secret to success.

I'm sure you've heard the expression, "Misery loves company." Well, I want to teach you a new one: "Misery may love company, but company does not love misery." Think about it! How do you feel after talking to someone who is feeling down? How about someone who is cheerful? Don't get me wrong—everyone is entitled to occasionally feel down, but the operative word is occasionally. So look for upbeat people, and be one yourself. It makes the world a better place.

Let me tell you about Ruth, who went away on vacation to visit her children and grandchildren. When she returned she was loving and full of life, but slowly this good feeling faded away. One day Ruth met Lucy at a convention, and the two hit it off. She told Lucy that she was going to spend the rest of the convention with her to stay away from negativity. When Lucy asked what had happened, Ruth gave her a simple explanation: Her children and grandchildren were healthy and happy, but her family and friends at home were constantly complaining. This was beginning to make her feel bad. Ruth was drawn to Lucy's positive outlook; it was contagious.

A good way to change any negative situation is to put the solution down on paper. For example, a coworker of mine was in a relationship that was bringing her down. After we spoke about it, she came up with these three ways to distance herself from the negativity:

- Prayer. She believed spiritual growth would give her strength.

- New unlisted telephone number. She ended the relationship but knew her ex-boyfriend would still call, and she would be tempted. She changed her number, and asked her secretary at the office not to put his calls through.

- New activity with her children. This would help keep her occupied as well as give her added time with her children.

Now it's your turn. Write down your thoughts and make them your reality.

Three ways I'm going to remove myself
from a negative situation to improve my self-esteem:

1. _____

_____

_____

2. _____

_____

_____

3. _____

_____

_____

Live how you would like to see yourself live

We all have made "I wish" statements: "I wish I could be as outgoing as Lee." "I wish I could speak as well as Patricia." "I wish I had Ann's knack for organization."

The truth is you can usually accomplish what you wish for—or at least improve yourself—but you have to do more than think it. What do I mean? Act it out, play the part. This doesn't mean that you should go through life emulating others. It means you should portray the traits that you wish you had.

For example, if you wish you had the ability to go out and meet people, go out and meet people. Act as if you were the type of person who would normally do this. In time it will become part of you, and your self-esteem will blossom. You are the builder of your self-confidence. Acting stronger allows you to see yourself being stronger; hence, showing that you can do it.

Don't tell me it's not as easy as it sounds, because it is. An associate once told me she believed her self-esteem would improve if she became more attractive. I encouraged her to do just that—become more attractive. We discussed what her idea of attractive was. She thought about it and decided she needed a new hairstyle and more modern clothes. She came to my office one day and I almost didn't recognize her. It wasn't so much her physical appearance, but she was beaming. In her case, the old adage is true: When you look good, you feel good.

A friend once told me she wished she was smart. I told her to change the "wish" to "will" and add "er," to say: "I will get smarter." Believe it or not, you are already what you want to be; therefore, you don't have to wish for it. You just may want to improve or add more to that characteristic.

Then I asked her, "What is a smarter person like?" (It is important to be specific when changing your behavior.) She answered that many people in her work community seemed to be highly educated and knew so much more than she did.

"How did they get that way," I asked.

"Probably by going to college," she replied.

"And what do people do in college?"

"They study, read and write," she said.

So, when I asked her to write down three things she would do to act as if she were smarter, she responded:

- Read more. She would begin reading the newspaper and novels.

- Listen to the news. She would pick up bits and pieces from the television or radio.

- Have conversations with others. She felt that smart people discussed important issues. So, armed with her knowledge of the news of the day, she began joining in on conversations.

The more she did this, the more she realized that she was just as smart as her coworkers. She just needed the confidence to show it.

Now it's up to you. Think about it and write down how the person you would like to be would act. Then go for it.

Three ways I am going to "act" my way toward better self-esteem:

1. _____

_____

_____

2. _____

_____

_____

3. _____

_____

_____

Feed yourself positive messages

Most people work hard at maintaining their lifestyle—shelter, food, transportation, etc. Why not employ yourself to maintain a healthy inner person that will shine as your outer person? You know what you need to pay your bills. Ask yourself what you need to do to make yourself feel good. Then do it. Tell yourself what you need to hear.

It will work if you believe it. You have the personal power to overcome obstacles. Tell yourself you are great and let those who think they can intimidate you see that they can't . . . because you are great.

We all run into people who just don't seem to like us. If someone is negative toward you, it has more to do with that person's self-image than anything about you. The important thing is liking yourself and treating yourself accordingly. How? You can start by eating wholesome foods, exercising and keeping a nice appearance. Remind yourself to do these things when you use your positive self-talk.

Here are a few suggestions:

- As you're getting ready for the day, look in the mirror and say, "I have a great smile."

- Maybe you're riding in the car and you were kind enough to let someone over during heavy traffic. Think to yourself. "I am a thoughtful person."

• Perhaps there is a project at work or school that has you busy. Remind yourself, "I can achieve my goals."

Your turn. Choose the statements that will be of most benefit to you and make a habit of saying them. Once you begin feeling good on the inside, it will show through on the outside.

Three positive statements I can say to myself to boost my self-esteem:

1. _____

_____

_____

2. _____

_____

_____

3. _____

_____

_____

MAINTAINING SELF-ESTEEM

So how do know when you have arrived? How do you know when your self-esteem will carry you through life's ups and downs? Actually, when it happens, there will be no doubt. This poem by contemporary California poet giovanni singleton says it eloquently. (See her bio after resources.)

my reflection

i do not trust math.
each year i mark its failings.
what is age really?

this i wonder while looking at my life,
its gracefulness and constant motion.

and as i examine its reflection, i give up
wanting to be taller. stature is not
a matter for a yard stick.

i no longer desire bigger breasts
for beauty is beyond measure, beyond
mere physicality.

i accept the fact that i cannot sing
yet there is a music within me. i hear
it playing wherever i am.

living keeps me sane. and now i no
longer need to search for myself.

i am a turtle inside a shell. i can see
the sky when the lights go dim and
i dance rather well.

— giovanni singleton

Once you hear the music inside yourself, you have discovered your self-esteem. You're on the right track, feeling good and loving it. Your big question is, "How do I stay this way?"

Basically, you maintain your self-esteem the same way you built it. First and foremost, you stay centered in your spirituality. Second, you stay away from negative situations and negative people. After all, you are a new person, who wants to look forward, not backward.

Then you get out there and move your body. Energy-exerting activities, such as walking, aerobics, dancing, yoga or martial arts help relieve tension, and do wonders for your self-image. The next thing you know, you will tone your body and improve the texture of your skin. The better your body feels, the better you feel about yourself.

Treat yourself to new or different things—a new hairstyle, a new restaurant; maybe just a different menu item in an old restaurant. Start small, then gradually build your way up to something more exciting. Always look for a new goal. It doesn't have to be monumental. It could be something as simple as rearranging the furniture or trying a new recipe. Just make sure it is something that makes you feel good. The activities at the end of this chapter will get you on the road to great self-esteem and keep you there.

Finally, if you feel you need additional help to tow the load, you may want to join a support group. You can talk about your problems and meet individuals who may have been in a similar situation. Realizing you are not alone may be just the boost you need. However, make sure it is a group that moves forward, not one that allows its members to wallow in their misery. This is not an overnight process. It takes time, and most of all, YOUR EFFORTS!

But remember, you're worth it.

Self-esteem Activities

ON A DAILY BASIS, PRACTICE THESE TECHNIQUES:

- Reaffirm your spiritual connection. (For me, just remembering just how much God loves me gives me a boost.)

- Remember to use positive self-talk. Say something positive about yourself, your day, and your life.

    "I am a kind and generous person."

    "My meeting today will be productive."

    "I am thankful that I have a home to live in."

- Turn negatives into positives.

  "It was terrible to have a car accident, but thank God no one was hurt."

  "Despite the frustrations of the morning, I got a lot accomplished today."

- Don't look back to negatives in your past, but forward to a positive future.

ON A WEEKLY BASIS:

Each week, choose one of the suggestions below and practice it. Check them off as you do them. The more you practice self-esteem building activities, the faster your self-confidence will grow. You are the only one that can make yourself feel better. Just do it.

- Set aside 20 minutes or so each day for spiritual reading or meditation. When you are centered, positivity flows from that center.

- Dedicate some of your prayer or meditation time to someone in need.

- Write down a positive thought and put it where you will read it every day.

- Smile at yourself in the mirror.

- Smile at others. Looking pleasant makes you feel pleasant, which will encourage others to be pleasant to you.

- Take a different route to work. Doing the same routine can put you in a rut. This is an easy way to do something different.

- Change your hairstyle—even if it's only adding bangs or parting your hair on the opposite side.

- Eat a healthy meal each day. Get in those five servings of fruits and vegetables. Once you discover that it's not so bad, you can try two healthy meals a day.

- Work out at least three times this week. This is possible! In the morning you can do stretches or run in place. At your desk, do tummy tucks. While watching television, squeeze a tennis ball or do leg lifts. Find a way to fit it in. You will feel great!

- Take a walk. Go to the park, the mall, your neighborhood and walk 20 minutes at least five times this week. It will get your blood flowing.

- Clean out your closet. Old clothes and depressing memories have got to go. Time to start wearing brighter clothes and making happier memories.

- Rearrange your furniture at home or spruce up your desk at the office. Sometimes making your surroundings look new changes your perspective.

- Go to the dentist for a cleaning. Since you're creating a new you, why not create a better smile to go with it.

- Pamper yourself. Get a manicure, a pedicure or a facial. Don't be discouraged if finances won't allow you to go to the salon. You can treat yourself at home. Take a long, soaking bath, then moisturize and polish your nails. Massage a moisturizer on your face, then cover with a warm, damp towel. Lay and relax for about 10 minutes. Rinse your face and feel refreshed.

- Buy your favorite song. Listening to music can be uplifting. If there's a song you always hum, purchase it and play it to perk you up. Or pull out a song you already have that makes you smile.

- Get up early and watch the sun rise. Appreciating nature and its beauty can put you more in touch with yourself. Then appreciate your own beauty and become at peace with yourself.

- Have a nice photograph taken of yourself. It doesn't have to be glamorous. It can be done by a friend or at the local department store. It's a real pick-me-up.

- Join a class. Learn something new for advancement or just for fun. It's another way to get out of the house. Check out your local community school.

- Greet someone you don't know. Your confidence should be building by now. Don't just walk up to any stranger, but perhaps someone new at work or in your class.

- Invite someone out. It doesn't have to be a "date." If you've met someone you would like to get to know better, ask him or her out for coffee, a movie, a church social.

- Learn something new each day. This could be anything that interests you, such as a new recipe for dinner or a new computer program at work. It could be finding out what interests the people you meet. It could even be learning a new word daily.

- Become a volunteer. Helping others can be a big help to you. When you make a difference in someone's life, you feel good about yourself. You will also discover that others have problems that make yours look small.

ON A LARGER SCALE

- List five positive accomplishments in your life. It could be as simple as helping a child ride a bike or contributing clothing to a local shelter. Even small gestures can make a big difference to someone in need.

- List at least two things, or people, that you look forward to and make them a part of your life. Visit the person who gives you a lift. Take more walks on the beach or at the park. Spend more time developing your spirituality. Things that you look forward to make you happy. Look forward to your happiness and go with it.

- Make a realistic goal for yourself, plan the steps and set up a timetable for achieving it. Be specific. Write down what you already know that will help you accomplish your goal and what else you will need. Visualize the end result and start working towards it. Don't give up until it's done. There is something about completing a project that makes you feel GREAT inside. That builds confidence, which definitely shows up on the outside.

Once you see that you can accomplish your goals, you can use this system to attack anything in your life. Make a list of the ways you would like to improve yourself or your life. Write down the steps you will need to take in order to accomplish each improvement. Follow those steps to your success!

YOU WILL SUCCEED, NO DOUBT!

If seeds of doubt begin to sprout, nip them in the bud. Listen to that uplifting song. Stand up and do a few jumping jacks. If you're confined to a chair, do some stretches. Say to yourself:

I AM THE GREATEST ME THAT WILL EVER BE!

Say it, believe it, and live it!

NO MORE PITY PARTIES FOR YOU!

It's time to make
the most of your life,
with or without
a romantic partner.

My 2¢

In my late teens and early 20s, whenever I didn't have a steady boyfriend, I felt that there was something missing in my life. At times I attempted to make relationships work when I knew they were doomed. I would go through seasons. Sometimes I was not involved in a relationship and felt wonderful. Then there were times I did not feel so wonderful and felt I needed to go out to find a mate. This is usually when I ran into someone not suitable—at least not suitable for me.

Simply put, I was a terrible single. One Friday night a girlfriend and I didn't have any dates or any prospects for that matter. We decided to go out together. While we were out she commented, "This is ridiculous! Two beautiful young ladies like ourselves out without dates." To myself I chuckled and thought, "This is ridiculous! Two intelligent young ladies like ourselves thinking a date is the answer."

When I thought about it, I realized I only thought I needed a man in my life when I was bored. When I was involved in activities, family events or social gatherings, I could laugh, talk, even flirt without thinking I should be with someone. On the other hand, if my calendar was open or a romantic holiday was around the corner, I would start thinking something was wrong. So, one of the best things I did was get involved in activities for myself and not for companionship. No more Pity Parties for me!

No more settling for me, either. Have you ever been with the wrong type of person for you just for the sake of having someone in your life? My mom helped me discover this one. I was dating a guy who was totally wrong for me. My mom told me to think about who I was and how this man would fit into the life I wanted. I thought about it and realized he was not what I wanted in a man. I also realized that sometimes it is better to be alone than to be with someone who does not understand you, someone who mistreats you or someone who only wants to use you.

What's the point? Having a companion who is not really a companion is worse than being alone. People view you as a desperate idiot. You're always making excuses for your mate's behavior. You try to convince your friends that he or she is worth it. Actually, you're just trying to convince yourself. Others know when you aren't content. It's written all over your face, just like it was written all over mine. Children even realize when you are in a bad space. Some grow up believing this is how life should be. Well, I wanted more than that for my future children—and for myself.

My philosophy came to be: It's worse to feel lonely when you are with someone than it is when you are alone.

Check out some of the advice I have given to readers:

Related Advice

Dear June: I'm writing to you as a single woman. Do you think I will ever find someone to love or get married? I'm 48, and it seems like when I get a friend they always end up hurting me. I'm a true person to my friends, but I'm the one who gets all the pain. —New Jersey

Dear New Jersey: I cannot say if you will find love and get married. But what's the big deal? You are not alone. There are millions of single people in the United States, more than one-third of the adult population. Many are leading happy and successful lives, because getting married is not the end-all, be-all of life. Realizing this is the first step to releasing your pain.

Now you need to focus on yourself and creating happiness from within. Pay more attention to being true to yourself. If you do not love, respect, and give yourself the best, how can you possibly expect anyone else to? Just take a good long look in the mirror at the person you should have been loving all these years.

• • •

Dear June: I have been with the same person for more than 10 years, and I just don't see it leading anywhere. We have children together, but he's always using the excuse that he's not ready to get married or he's too young to get married. I feel this is an important part of the relationship. I also feel I have been giving too much of myself and it's not leading to anything. Should I pursue something else? —N. Miami

Dear N. Miami: Yes! You should pursue something else—YOURSELF! If you feel marriage is an important part of the relationship and he does not, then obviously you are on two different wavelengths. This probably means you are separated on other issues as well. My mother always says if a relationship is not progressing the way you would like it to in a year, perhaps you should re-evaluate the relationship. I would add that you should also re-evaluate yourself. If you feel your needs and wants are not being met, then you need to ask these two questions: What is so great about him that I cannot live without him? What is so terrible about myself that I cannot live alone?

• • •

Dear June: I am a 21-year-old female who was dating one of the best men you can find. We recently broke up and when he heard I was with someone else, he slapped me. He apologized, and I really felt his sympathy was sincere. Do you think that's sign of danger? Should I be careful of this guy? —Lauderhill, FL

Dear Lauderhill: Let me get straight to the point: If he slapped you, he is NOT one of the best men you can find. Yes, I think that is a sign of danger. Yes, you should be careful of this guy and stay as far away from him as you can.

• • •

Dear June: I have to come realize that I should live without the man I have been seeing due to his physical aggression. What can I do to keep my mind from being focused on him? I know this is not what's best for me, but I have to see him two or three times a week at college.

— Please Help

Dear Help: I know this is a difficult situation. However, you were strong enough to pull yourself away from him physically, so I am sure you can find enough strength to pull away from him emotionally, as well. Here are some tips to remember: You are always much too busy to have a conversation or a cup of coffee with him. There are more fish in the sea; go get some bait and catch one. Better yet, forget the fish for now and focus on the fisherwoman. Start a study group, join a hobby group or just concentrate on your college education. Work on your qualities and ways you can develop your skills. Along the way, you will find an even better person to focus upon—YOU.

• • •

Dear June: I need your help. I just started living with my boyfriend. This is our second try; we have lived together before. Our relationship has lasted off and on for about six years. I love him, but I am not in love with him. We both agreed to try to rekindle the magic, but after only two weeks he has slipped back into some old habits and I am now reminded of why I asked him to leave the first time. There are some things that have improved about him, like finances, but other things remain the same. Do you think I am giving up too soon?   —Miramar, FL

Dear Miramar: You have been off and on with this guy for about six years. Do I think that you are giving up too soon? Wait! Let me think about it. All right, NO, I DO NOT!

If the relationship has not worked out in six years, what makes you think it's going to change now? I hope you do not believe that you can build an alliance just because of an improvement in the financial situation. It is time for you to make a conscious decision. Do you want to sell yourself out for money—someone else's money at that? Or do you want to create a better life for yourself? You can improve your own financial situation. If he is the one with the finances, then he may decide to do what he wants with the money and leave you out in the cold. Give him up and move on.

The Heart of the Matter

*Y*our self-esteem is high. You say, "Hey, I'm not so bad. In fact, I'm a pretty great person. So, why am I still single?"

To that I say: Make the best of where you are today—enjoy being single. And I will show you how.

As I see it, there are three types of singles, and each faces specific challenges.

- Those who have never been married

- Those who are divorced

- Those who only THINK they are in a relationship

Those of you who have never been married may feel you have been left out of the game. As I said before, you are not alone—not by far—with more than one-third of the American adult population in the same boat with you. Many singles live full, happy well-adjusted lives.

The "now I'm single because I'm divorced" group often has a tough time moving on. Although it is painful, you can turn this situation into a growing experience. Once you take the time to focus on yourself, it will ease the heartbreak of a broken relationship.

Then there is the third group—those of you who only *think* you are in a relationship. But truthfully, you don't really think that, do you? A relationship involves two people who care about each other in a give-and-take situation. But, come on, you know you're only there so you can say, "I have somebody." Please! Give it a rest! It's more embarrassing to make up excuses about a one-sided relationship than to show the world how successful you can be as a single.

Sure you want companionship—we all do! Does that mean you cannot enjoy yourself unless you have a romantic companion? Of course not. Take advantage of this time to work on yourself. Here are the steps that will guide you in your path:

Steps to successful singlehood:

1. HAVE A GOOD RELATIONSHIP WITH YOURSELF.

Have there been times when you dated someone just because it was better than being lonely? He or she did not really interest you, but, hey, it beats a blank. Well, the question is, does it really? The relationship surely ended—or will end—in a dead end. You probably thought you could make it work, or at least make the best out of it. Sorry, it just doesn't work that way, does it?

If you knew yourself a little better, you would have known it wasn't going to lead anywhere. So spend some time discovering who you are. Think about the people and traits you value in life, your hopes and dreams and ambitions. This will help you know your self-worth, so you'll be less likely to sacrifice your values to be with someone who does not support them.

Go places and enjoy your own company, as opposed to waiting for someone to keep you company. When you feel comfortable with yourself, lack of a relationship will not consume you.

Appreciate yourself enough to keep your appearance at its best. Just because you don't have a date on Saturday night doesn't mean you have to curl up in front of the television with a bag of cheese puffs and a half-gallon of rocky road ice cream. A successful single is a healthy single who eats right and keeps alcohol and other harmful substances at a distance. A healthy diet has a huge impact, not only on your physical well-being, but also your mental state.

It helps create a health cycle: When you take care of yourself, you feel better, you feel more secure and confident and you like yourself better—so you want to continue to take better care of yourself and your life.

You'll be happier, more at peace, and as an added benefit, you will better know what you want in a partner, should the right one come along.

A successful single is a physically and mentally well-adjusted single.

2. DEVELOP SEVERAL INTERESTS.

There's a distinct advantage to being single: You don't have to figure a mate's needs into your schedule. Your time is truly your time—you need not worry about spending too much time away from home. Take advantage of this by going back to school or learning a new skill. You can travel without having to correlate your schedule with someone else's schedule.

Getting out and doing things improves your mental state and gives you the opportunity to meet others with the same interests. It widens your circle of associates. It also gives you the opportunity to have fun and do things you may not normally do. Nothing increases loneliness more than doing nothing.

Remember Mary from Chapter 1—the woman who let a man take over her life? She decided to make some changes and began attending social functions relating to her job. She met several goal-oriented, positive people. Some were professional women who were single and happy. As she talked with them, she realized they had goals and other priorities besides having a mate. The thought of pursuing something for herself had never occurred to her.

Soon she realized that her mate was not spending that much time with her, which left her pretty much alone anyway. She ended her tumultuous relationship.

Then Mary, who already had a two-year degree, went back to school to complete her bachelor's degree.

She was promoted from administrative assistant to departmental manager. She dates periodically, but feels just as comfortable going out alone. She never realized that she could be content without being committed to a relationship.

To jump-start your life, first set your goals. This is essential not only for singles, but for everyone in all stages of life. Goals motivate you and keep you in a positive mode. Make a list of what you would like to accomplish, prioritize, then write down what is necessary for you to accomplish your goals. Finally, decide your plan of action and write it down so you can visualize what you need to do. Then GO FOR IT!

Remember, you are a successful single—there is no one standing in your way.

You can start by planning your week. Make it flexible in the event a better offer comes along. Here is an example:

Mon.	Work, Spa, Dinner, Pottery Class
Tues.	Work, Laundry, Music Lesson, Dinner
Wed.	Work, Spa, Dinner, Bible Study
Thurs.	Work, Early Bird Special, TV w/Friends
Fri.	Work, Spa, Dinner, Sports Event
Sat.	Breakfast, Art Festival, Rest, Jazz Night
Sun.	Breakfast, Church, Dinner, Family Time

This is just one example. I realize that there are many individuals who do not work a "Monday through Friday, 9 to 5" job. Arrange your schedule chart to suit your needs. If you bore easily, change it often. What is most important is that you keep yourself on track and involved with the world.

3. HAVE HEALTHY WAYS OF EXPRESSING YOUR SEXUALITY.

Being a successful single means having self-respect and self-control when it comes to sexuality. Sometimes, out of loneliness, singles end up in unhealthy sexual liaisons. We've all seen it, heard about it or lived it: a night out at the club, too much drinking, going home with near strangers. Some people call it partying; I call it asking for trouble.

Just because you meet someone who appears very interested in you and tells you what you want to hear does not mean you should have sex with that person. Just because you are lonely and haven't had an intimate partner in what seems like forever, does not mean you should pick up a one-night stand. Aside from the numerous diseases you could contract (that a condom does not always protect against), it's torment on your emotional state. Your reputation can get raked over the coals, and your self-esteem can get flushed down the toilet. Find ways to occupy your time and exert your energy that will contribute to your mental and physical well-being.

I worked in a hospital once and a young man came in with a sexually transmitted disease (STD). Needless to say, he was very uncomfortable. During treatment the attending nurse explained appropriate sexual behavior and the benefits of safe sex. In less than a month, he was back with another STD. His rationale was that he was lonely and wanted companionship. The nurse warned him more sternly. "If you think you're lonely now," she told him, "wait until you end up admitted to the hospital with a deadly sexually transmitted disease."

Please remember that a successful single is a cautious single.

4. DEVELOP A POSITIVE SUPPORT NETWORK (PSN).

It's your birthday or the holidays, and you wish you had a mate to celebrate with. Do you sit and mope and wallow in your misery? Or do you go out and at least make an attempt to enjoy yourself?

Yeah, yeah, you've heard it all before—go out with family and friends. Furthermore, you have tried it, but it's just not the same.

You're right, it's not the same. It's just your good fortune that there are people out there who are willing to spend their valuable time to make special days better for you. Be thankful, and not just on Thanksgiving Day. Celebrating with family and friends is nearly always better than nothing, and it can be really fun—if you can just find time to stop moping about your lack of relationship.

The first step in developing your PSN is getting in touch with your spiritual anchor, through prayer, reading or joining a spiritual community. Discovering or recovering that inner strength will keep you from falling into harmful behaviors. It will also help you focus on the positive, rather than the negative.

The next step is focusing on the friends and family members who truly give you support. Keep in regular contact with them, not only for companionship but also for safety. Tell them where you are going and with whom. Always leave them your date's name, address, car make and anything else you can think of. There should be a select group in your PSN that you can call any time, day or night, to share information. (For more on your Positive Support Network, see Chapter 4.)

A successful single is a safe single.

Let me elaborate on friendship. I talked earlier about widening your circle of associates. I use this term because friendship requires a special bond between people. We should be aware of the differences between someone we associate with and someone who really cares enough to be considered a true friend.

So many times single people surround themselves with other singles who are unhappy about their situation. How can that possibly encourage you? Ever heard the expression, "All men are dogs?" Who do you think started this expression? I could be wrong, but I can imagine it was a bunch of lonely single women complaining about men.

And men, don't think you are off the hook. What about, "All the good women are married"? or "All women are . . ."

Well, you get the picture. When singles get together and commiserate, the opposite sex doesn't have a fighting chance. Doing the group thing can turn into a giant Pity Party. Sometimes, you're better off alone.

Moving in packs can also thwart opportunities to meet a mate. Think back to a time you have been to a party with three or four people of the same sex. You may have been attracted to someone, but that someone probably did not approach you because your cohorts were around. Or maybe you and a friend were both attracted to the same person, or someone you were interested in was attracted to your friend. These are awkward situations. You either end up being distraught because you do not want to offend anyone or because someone offended you.

Here's a suggestion. If you go to a party with a group, agree to mingle separately. Arrange to check in with each other periodically; and also leave together. That's right . . . leave together. If you and the person you meet really want to take things a step further, you can arrange to get in touch later.

5. HAVE HIGH STANDARDS.

Know what you want from yourself and from a mate, and don't settle for less. As I stated earlier: YOU ARE A SUCCESSFUL SINGLE! DON'T LET ANYONE STAND IN YOUR WAY—ESPECIALLY THAT PERSON IN THE MIRROR.

The more you know about yourself and what you like to do, the more you can determine what you expect from companionship. If you know yourself, you will not settle for someone who is not on the same wavelength, someone who may interfere with you achieving your goals.

Also, don't allow yourself to be in a relationship just because it seems like the "right thing" to do. For example, single parents may marry so their children will have two parents. Yes, it is great to have two parents, but if the two parents are not of the same accord, it can do great damage to children, not to mention the adults. Make sure you consider all the factors before jumping into a relationship.

Finally, don't be consumed with having a companion. Ever known someone who jumped into a new relationship before the last one was cold? Don't let this be you. If it is, you need to complete all the steps in Chapter 1. Sometimes it is better to be involved with a pet, hobby or another activity rather than an unpleasant and/or unhealthy relationship. Know and like yourself enough that you can be comfortable being alone. In simple terms, don't be desperate.

Answering the following questions can help you figure out who you are and what you want out of life.

Self-Search

- Do you work more than one job?

- Do you work beyond your normal working hours more than twice a week?

- Do you drink alcohol or take other harmful substances as part of your recreational activities?

- Do you have a lot of associates?

- Do you need more than one or two people with you in order to have a good time?

- Have your friends gotten you in trouble within the last year?

- Do you usually choose to stay home when you don't have a date?

- Do you sacrifice your good time to please a companion?

- Do you let others choose the events when going out?

- Are you uncertain what it is you like to do?

- Do you spend more time working on a date/mate than accomplishing your goals?

If you answered yes to any of these questions, explain why. For example, "Substance abuse is part of my recreational activity because my friends do it and it helps me deal with my loneliness" or "I have a lot of associates because I have a great personality and make friends easily."

IT'S IMPORTANT THAT YOU'RE HONEST WITH YOURSELF!

If you have been honest, you will find patterns. Once you understand these patterns, you will be able to see the ones that are moving you forward, as well as the ones that are holding you back. Then you will hold the key that opens the door to positive changes in your life.

Here are some possible patterns:

- You always meet your dates while partying, then you get upset when your mate continues to party instead of spending quality time with you.

- You think that nice people aren't assertive, so you end up in verbally or physically abusive relationships.

Use your self search answers to design a new road map.

IF I WERE A...

To further explore your character and personality, use the following list of topics and fill in the blanks of this sentence.

If I were a _____ I would be a _____ because _____.

For example, if I were a *flower,* I would be a *daisy* because *it's bright and easy, not stiff and formal like a rose or orchid.*

Now it's your turn, and here's your list:

flower	**jewelry**	**color**
food	**animal**	**furniture**
car	**school**	**boat**
book	**shoe**	**radio station**
song	**item of clothing**	

Review the items you've chosen (such as "daisy") with your "because" answers to discover what they have in common. Do your answers appear to be the norm? Extremely bold? Carefully chosen? Are all your answers similar? Not only should you learn something about yourself, but about the way you have been choosing your mates.

Doing the following exercise can help you understand what you're looking for in a relationship.

MATE INVENTORY

- Write down everything that you want in a mate. In other words, if you could create your dream mate, what qualities would he or she have. You don't have to be realistic here. The sky's the limit.

- Make a copy of it.

- On the original version, draw a line through the qualities that you consider fantastic, but make sure you can still read them.

- Next draw a circle around the qualities that would be really nice, but that you could live without.

- Now highlight the qualities that are required — you definitely need these in a mate.

- Take the copy of your list and check off the qualities your last two mates had, then compare it to the highlighted qualities on the original.

Did your last couple of mates fit the bill, or have you been settling? Perhaps they had some of the qualities that were crossed from your list, so you accepted those over the more important ones. Know what you want, and don't sell yourself short.

GETTING THROUGH THE HOLIDAY BLUES

Do you get through most of the year OK, but the holidays really wallop you? The best way to get through the holiday blues is to still celebrate those special days, regardless of your romantic social life. Here's how:

Become a volunteer!

Stop feeling sorry for yourself and do something to help others less fortunate. Maybe you don't have a mate, but if you still have your senses, a place to live and food to eat, you have a lot for which to be thankful. There are many organizations such as children's hospitals, veteran's associations, soup kitchens, etc. that are looking for individuals to share a little of their time. Do something good for someone else and feel good about yourself.

Have a party!

Remember, you are not the only single out there. Invite other singles—and couples, too—to celebrate with you. Encourage them to bring friends and relatives that you may not know. This gives you the opportunity to have a good time and possibly meet new people. Invite people you have met at all those new classes you've been taking, or from the new group you've joined.

Life is what you make of it. Wouldn't you rather make it fun?

Rhythmic, Romantic, Roaring Relationships

Romantic relationships
can be tricky,
but they can also be
a lot of fun.

My 2¢

$\mathcal{I}$'ve learned relationships can be tricky from my own relationship with my husband. Why tricky? Because Tim and I sometimes go overboard trying to please each other and read each other's mind. Then we laugh about it—that's the fun part. We try to find humor or romance in situations that would normally be a little stressful.

The most memorable example of this happened when we were dating. Tim had car trouble, so I joined him while he waited for the tow truck. As we sat there, he turned and said to me, "Can this constitute a romantic moment?" I thought he was crazy until he pulled out the ring box and told me he wanted to marry me. Who said breakdowns are not romantic? Throughout our marriage, we have continued the tradition of finding romance and laughter in everyday life.

I call this chapter "Rhythmic, Romantic, Roaring Relationships" because it's important to have a roaring good time with your significant other, even—no, especially—when the situation is less than perfect—then the rhythm and romance will follow. I feel that the positive should outweigh the negative a hundred times over. If it doesn't, you're spinning your wheels.

Tim and I work at keeping our relationship fresh and fun, and it's work we love to do. A friend once asked when our honeymoon was going to end. My answer is probably never, because if one ends, we pick up and go on another. It's not that Tim and I are so special, it's that we have decided that we want to have a trusting, joyful relationship, and we are willing to do what it takes to keep it that way.

Someone once asked me why she couldn't find a man to treat her as my husband treats me. My response was, "You don't want a man who treats you that way. If you did, you would not settle for less." As we discussed in the previous chapter, to know what you want in a mate you have to know yourself. My dad always said, "Choose a date that will be a good mate." I knew what my requirements were. My husband fit the bill.

When Tim and I were dating, we discussed exactly what we wanted and expected from a relationship openly and honestly. We then had to decide in which areas we were willing to bend or not bend. If you are straight about what you want from the beginning, you save a lot of time, and you can move on to a more enjoyable part of the relationship.

It helps to look at relationships that have worked well. My parents were married more than 40 years before my dad passed away two years ago. Their relationship was so strong sometimes it seemed as if they were still dating. They found a way to develop individually while staying committed to each other. This is how a relationship should be. If your parents did not have a healthy relationship, you can start a new tradition. Find a couple in a loving, long-term marriage. Ask them how they did it. Make them your model for success.

From my column, here is more advice regarding relationships:

Related Advice

Dear June: My husband and I have three children in their preteens. We love them and often do things as a family, including vacations. This year we want to do something special with just the two of us, but are not sure it would be right to leave the children behind for about a week. Both our parents will be happy to oblige, as they have kept them for our weekend trips. Do you think a week is too long to go away without the children? —Doting parents, Fort Lauderdale, FL

Dear Doting: If you don't take time for yourselves, how can you maintain that positive energy for your children? A week is not too long to go away without your children when you have appropriate care for them. You are lucky to have trustworthy, caring parents who are willing to help you. I'm sure after rearing children of their own, they understand parents need a vacation for themselves. So, enjoy your trip, and make sure to bring lots of souvenirs back for your parents and children.

• • •

Dear June: My husband of 13½ years has a buddy who recently got divorced after 13 years of marriage. Since then we have been having problems because my husband comes home late saying that his buddy is suicidal and needs him. Three weeks ago my husband came home at 1 A.M. with perfume all over his shirt. He told me he ran into a lot of people while he and his buddy were at a nightclub. Then he told me he was dancing with a girl, after I didn't swallow the first story. I told him to choose between his buddy and me, because it seems he wants our marriage to fail, too. Am I wrong or selfish for not wanting him around my husband?

— Heartbroken

Dear Heartbroken: This must be a trying situation for you, but you need to calmly approach your husband to settle this issue. I suggest you begin by working out a compromise. For example, set times or schedules to give the two of you more time together, and use the time together wisely. What do I mean?

After 13 years of marriage, you may need to discover ways to rekindle the flame. Use your imagination. Make him aware that you want to be with him. If he wants to go dancing, then tell him you would love to go with him.

You are not wrong or selfish, but your husband's buddy is. You are also right that your husband is responsible for himself and needs to make a choice. If he doesn't come around, you will have to make the choice for him and do what is best for you.

• • •

Dear June: It has been said that "opposites attract" in a relationship. How can a bond or closeness be formed between two people who are so different? —Interested

Dear Interested: Yes, that is a common cliché. In many instances, it may appear to be true. For example, my husband always says that I am what he is not. It seems that when opposites attract, they benefit from the traits of their significant other or complement each other. I still feel, however, there has to be some commonality between individuals to make a strong, long-lasting relationship.

• • •

Dear June: My wife complains that I work too much, but someone has to pay the bills. I try to spend as much time as possible with her and the kids, but I am an independent contractor. So, when duty calls, I have to answer. I wish I could get her to understand that I do this because I love her and want to provide for her. Any suggestions? —Working Husband

Dear Working: I've heard many people in their final days of life talk about things they wish they had done. Not one of them mentioned more time at work. Make sure your schedule is in line with your values.

If work occasionally gobbles up your time, making the time you have with your loved ones special can help. Take her out for a nice dinner, have a romantic weekend away, plan a play day with the whole family. Discuss your ideas with your wife and follow through. You won't regret it. But you may regret your years as a workaholic.

The Heart of the Matter

Flowers, candy, soft music, candlelight. These images come to mind when we think of romance, and they certainly are wonderful. But true romance takes more than sensual gifts and mood-setters.

It all starts, of course, with love. I am not talking about being "in love," because that is only one piece of a big picture. Being in love can be a wonderful experience, but it can also cloud the common sense of the most intelligent person. For love to last, you must get to know and love your mate as you would a close personal friend, before you become romantic partners.

Mary learned this lesson through a series of failed relationships. She and her dates didn't get to know one another before they "fell" into romance. Over time, the attraction ended because the communication never started. Mary learned not to commit herself right away. She put romance on the back burner and became friends with the men she dated. If there was no connection, she moved on. She was finally on the way to a lasting romantic relationship.

Of course, for Mary to be comfortable with a loving relationship, she had to first love herself. It all keeps coming back to self-esteem, doesn't it? If you don't value yourself and have standards, you will not consider yourself worthy of love. You will choose a partner who fits your negative view of yourself. That partner, sensing that you are unsure of yourself, will be able to walk all over you. That happened to Mary before she worked on her self-esteem.

On the other hand, if you believe in, care for and respect yourself, you will find a mate who believes in, cares for and respects you. (Now don't go overboard. I'm not saying that you should have a superior attitude—that is actually a sign of insecurity, and it will only push others away.)

When you have good self-esteem, you will be approachable and lovable. You just won't jump at every offer.

Once you have grown to know and love someone as a friend, you will know if you should take the relationship to the next step. This takes time and much consideration, but finding the relationship that's right for you is worth the effort. When you have found the person who is right for you, three factors will keep the relationship strong and loving:

- Trust through honest communication

- Commitment: fidelity and moral support

• Passionate feelings that result in physical intimacy

Let's take a further look at these elements.

Without honesty there can be no trust. Without communication, there can be no trust. Let's say you have something on your mind. Maybe it's something major haunting you from your past . . . maybe it's really no big deal—just a toe ache. Your mate asks what's going on, but you shrug it off in order not to cause your mate concern. Now your partner starts to imagine the worst. What happens next? You start going back and forth, and it turns into a major discussion. What a waste of time! Keeping the lines of communication open will build a more trusting relationship, and save you a lot of aggravation.

Do you know how much trouble and energy I've saved by just saying what's on my mind? Tons! I'm not talking about being rude, just honest about what you are feeling or about situations you may be going through. If you are open with your mate, your mate more likely will be open with you.

As for commitment, it's more than remaining faithful—refraining from sexual relations with another person. It also means you will stand by your partner and give your full support. If by chance your mate becomes ill or unable to perform physically, you don't dart out on the relationship. Commitment means you will hang in there to support your mate through trying times.

In regard to intimacy, if you don't have passionate feelings and a true desire to be intimate with your partner, there is no true romantic relationship. Such a situation increases the chance of infidelity, which breaches the commitment and ruins the trust.

So what happens if you are no longer attracted to your partner? Determine why. Usually it's more than just physical appearance. Mental and emotional factors may come into play. The moral support once given could be gone. These situations need to be discussed—and sometimes a couple may need counseling—which leads back to communication.

A co-worker once told me that her husband had complained the she was not as affectionate as she once was. She told me he wasn't as attentive as he once was. If he would just call to say "hello" or "I love you," she said, she would be eager to be with him when they were at home. I told her she needed to tell him the same thing she told me. They needed to discuss the situation to find a solution.

I'm sure you've heard many times that communication is the key to a relationship. It's true—and it's the key to sexual intimacy, as well. These four rules for relationship communication will help you keep the information—and the love—flowing.

1. SPEAK AND LISTEN WITH AN OPEN HEART AND OPEN MIND.

One of the worst things you can say to your mate is, "If you love me, you would . . ." That puts contingencies on the relationship. It's a quick way to kill an open discussion. The other person could respond, "If you loved me, you wouldn't ask me to . . ."

When you care about someone, it's your responsibility to hear his or her needs just as you want them to hear yours. Keeping an open mind and speaking frankly about your feelings will allow you to solve problems rationally and logically.

Many times we ladies wait for our man to romance us, and we expect them to know what we want. My husband says women want their men to be mind readers. Well, he says, most are not. So, ladies we have to be realistic and spill our guts. There is absolutely nothing wrong with having a conversation to explain how you feel and what your desires are.

While we're on the subject, we ladies can do some romancing, too. Treat him as you would like to be treated, and I'll bet he gets the picture. If he doesn't, TELL HIM.

Opening the lines of communication does not mean the two of you will agree on every subject—after all, you are not clones. With a little work, however, you will find that your differing traits and views can complement one another. For example, an outgoing mate could encourage a shy mate to explore events that otherwise he or she may not have tried. Note I said encourage, not force.

With your open heart, you will care enough about your mate to think with an open mind. This way, you can avoid undue confrontation, even if you don't agree on a particular subject. My parents used the term "agree to disagree." In other words, they didn't always see eye to eye, but they accepted that and respected the other's opinion.

If you can laugh about your disagreements, that's even better. My husband and I were riding in the car a few months after we married. I was upset about a rude employee in a department store. Tim thought I was overreacting. As a newlywed, I thought he should agree with everything I said. As a mature adult, I should have known better. After we discussed the situation, Tim told me to "Let it go, blow it out." So, I rolled down the window and started blowing. He asked what I was doing. I told him, "Blowing it out." We laughed and started a tradition. Start your own tradition to let off steam during disagreements.

2. HONESTY DOES NOT MEAN CRUELTY.

During difficult conversations, you should always remember that you love and care for one another. There are ways to discuss confrontational issues without attacking or accusing your partner. Use "I feel" statements to express what's in your heart or on your mind. Instead of saying, "You are spending too much time at work," say, "I feel lonely at night when you work so late."

Showing often works better than telling. Men, if you want her to be sexy, give her lingerie. If you want her to cook fancy dinners more often, volunteer to do the grocery shopping and prepare a sumptuous meal together. Women, if you want him to spend more time with you, design it. Farm the kids out to trustworthy caregivers, make a path of roses leading from the front door to the candle-lit bathtub, filled with bubbles—and you, of course.

Have conversations, not arguments. Blow kisses instead of throwing snide remarks. Proverbs chapter 21, verse 19 says, "It is better to dwell in the wilderness, than with a contentious and an angry woman." We don't want our men to feel this way about us, do we?

For men, Ephesians chapter 5, verse 28 says, "So ought men to love their wives as their own bodies. He that loveth his wife loveth himself." So, the way you treat her shows how you feel about yourself.

3. TALK AND LISTEN, BUT DON'T TOUCH . . . YET.

Knowing you can communicate honestly gives you a trusting bond, which in turns gives you a better relationship. This improves your intimate times.

If you cannot trust or communicate with your partner, you don't have a true passionate relationship—you have a fling. Flings are health hazards. Avoid them like the plague. Stick to a monogamous relationship and enjoy life a little longer.

Sexual intimacy should be the result of passionate feelings for your mate. In other words, it should not be a part of your duties. If it is, you need to work at improving this area of your life. I am a firm believer that sex needs to be discussed. Find out what lights your mate's fire. Find out what does not. Make time to explore each other's likes and dislikes.

First, have a discussion about what you already know turns you on and what turns you off. For example, if you like to be kissed on the back of the neck, remind your mate of that. Or, if tickling doesn't work as foreplay for you, explain that. Each of you should take a turn. Next, each mate should take a turn to ask questions or make suggestions. For instance, coming home during lunch for a quickie could make your day. Suggest it to your mate. You can even write down your ideas and exchange them to plan surprises for each other.

Finally, if there are certain ideas you would like to try, go ahead. This is your time to touch and explore. Make it fun, laugh, and enjoy each other's company. A couple who is committed to each other will find time to discover what makes the other happy emotionally and physically.

4. YOUR RELATIONSHIP IS NOBODY'S BUSINESS BUT YOURS.

Talking too much about your relationship to outsiders can create problems. Let's say you had a disagreement with your partner, and you broadcast it to anyone who will listen. Of course, it's a one-sided story and your friends support you. Then you make up with your mate, and your friends think you're crazy for staying in the relationship. Your mate is ticked because your friends are being distant, and he is wondering how much you can be trusted. You don't want to hear criticism from your friends, but, hey, you started it. Now you have to patch things up with your mate. If you had kept your mouth shut and worked it out with your partner in the first place, you wouldn't be in this pickle.

Or let's say you bragged about how great your lover is. Now he or she is being tempted by someone in your own back yard who wants a closer look. What goes on behind closed doors is between you and your mate. If you spill the beans, you may have to pick them up.

You and your partner should be able to share information without fear that it will be discussed with anyone else. You should be each other's confidant—trusting and depending on each other more than outside sources.

That trust can also be a source of a lot of fun, as you develop your own inside jokes. I'm talking about those "you had to be there" laughs. What better way to have a roaring good time with your mate than sharing in laughter that only the two of you understand.

Summing it all up, to have a complete relation-ship, you must have trust developed through honest communication. You must be committed to one another, being faithful and supportive. You must share your passion through physical intimacy.

Nope, you can't have one or two without the other. You see, you can trust your mate, but if there is no intimacy or commitment, then there is no romantic relationship. Basically, you have a room-mate. And if you have intimacy without trust or com-mitment, you have nothing more than a fling.

You have great self-esteem and have built a stronger inner self. You certainly won't settle for less than a great relationship now. Good for you . . . and good for your mate!

Relationship Activities

REMEMBER WHO YOU LOVE

Your mate is a good person who really cares for you; still, you're frustrated by some annoying habit. He always picks his teeth after he eats, or she wears old ratty T-shirts to bed. First of all, keep in mind this thought: There are many people who wish they still had their mate around to annoy them.

Make a list of the things you like about your mate and what attracted you at the beginning of the relationship. At least three times a week use this list to deliver a positive statement to your mate. For example, "Your smile is as warm and bright as the day we met."

One more thought: Deliver a heartfelt "I LOVE YOU!" at least once a day.

START A GOOD TIME TRADITION

Try to find something you will both enjoy that you can learn together. For instance, if you both enjoy big band music, take ballroom dancing lessons.

If you have trouble finding common ground on a activity, maybe you can both bend a little. If you like tennis and your mate likes basketball, teach each other. At least once a month, have a good time together learning the other's sport.

THE RELATIONSHIP GAME

The object of this game is to find out as much about your partner as you can in a fun and loving manner. Part of the fun is that you and your partner make the game yourself.

What you need:

- pack of index cards

- pen for each partner

- score tokens (poker chips, coins, raisins, nuts, cookies)

- a list of simple prizes made by each player (back rub, lunch date, kitchen duty for a week)

- list of categories (food, money, romantic ideas, home & garden, leisure activities)

Preparation: Each player writes questions about himself or herself on the index cards to ask the partner. They can be open questions, true/false, fill-in-the-blank or multiple choice. Try to think of questions that will reveal something about yourself, your interests, goals or desires.

Here are some samples.

- Fill-in blank: June's favorite meal is _____.

- Multiple choice: If June only had $5 until payday, she would

  a) buy a McDonald's meal

  b) hold onto it as long as possible

  c) get a surprise for Tim

- Open question: What's June's idea of a romantic night?

- True/false: June would like to live in a house with a big back yard for gardening.

These are basic questions just to get you started. You also could include news events, trivia and questions that are more intimate. Try to get at least 10 questions, with two or three questions from each category you choose.

Rules:

- A lot of fun and smiling.

- Absolutely no arguing. This is to learn about your partner, not be upset because he/she gives a wrong answer.

- Wait silently until your partner has completed his/her answer before responding.

How to Play: Place the card stacks on the table. You can do one category at a time or mix the categories together. Each person picks one card at a time from the stack created by the other person and answers the question. If the answer is correct, the player gets a token. If the answer is incorrect, the other partner should give the correct answer. (This is the time to talk and laugh and have a good time.) The next person then takes a turn. The person with the most tokens will choose one of the prizes from his/her list.

BEDROOM GAMES

- Have a picnic in bed wearing intimate outfits— you could even dress as you would for a picnic, but with a few sensual adaptations. Spread a feast of finger foods—appetizers, grapes, strawberries, chocolates—and feed each other.

- Play Simon Says—the intimate version. Take turns using the command to tell your partner what you want him or her to do. Simon says, walk slowly to me. Simon says, remove your robe. Simon says . . . well, I think you get the picture. At least, I hope you do.

  GO TO IT AND REMEMBER TO HAVE FUN!!!

At the End
of Your Rope?
Get a Grip!

"That girl don't stay down
for long."
That's what my dad
told my mother about me
when I was in my early 20s.

My 2¢

$\mathcal{F}$or most of my life, I have had a fairly buoyant personality. When Tim and I first got together, I was a pretty happy-go-lucky person. I laughed a lot, and if something didn't go exactly right, I could shrug it off. This was part of what attracted him to me.

In my early 30s, however, I went through a physical and emotional trauma that did get me down. I first noticed it at my job. I could work well in the morning, but after lunch, forget about it. I was too tired to be productive. I also suffered from employee burnout and felt I couldn't get a grip on my life.

One day, I lost it, and starting crying a lot and retreating into my shell. I was depressed and "just couldn't be bothered," as my best girlfriend would say. My husband was really confused by this and called my mother—I am grateful they have a good relationship. She told him not to worry, that I would be all right. Mom was right. Tim and I figured it was just my time of the month. After a while, the blue, stressed-out feeling began to cloud my moods more than once a month, and I was feeding the problem.

Many times we don't even realize that we're feeding the problem. Tim says it's like a person with a cold who feels hot from a fever, so she sleeps with the fan blowing on her all night. The next morning, the fever is worse, so she sits in a tub of cold water and gets even worse. It's not until she begins taking appropriate steps—drinking plenty of fluids, getting plenty of rest, keeping warm—that she begins to feel better.

At first, I was moping around the house a lot, eating only junk or nothing at all. I was making the problem worse by doing the opposite of what I needed. After a while, I woke up and realized I couldn't go around losing it with students, and I had my advice column to do, as well as other projects. Most importantly, I didn't want to jeopardize the great relationship my husband and I had. So I simply had to find a way out of the malaise that had overtaken me. I decided to do some research, through books on physical and mental well-being and the Internet, to determine how I could make myself feel better.

The way I see it, we all have two choices when facing life's disappointments: wallow in self-pity and walk around with a dark cloud hanging over our heads, or move forward. So I'm sharing with you steps that helped me keep it together. I hope they will help you when you encounter a bump in the road—or even a mountain.

My problem turned out to be physically based. After I began having pain in my abdomen, I went to the doctor and had a sonogram. The diagnosis was unusual cysts on my ovaries, among other problems. Eventually I had to have surgery to correct the problem.

Regardless of the source of depression, physical or mental, it's real and you must get to the bottom of it to get well. I needed medical help. For many, psychological help is needed. The important point here is not to ignore persistent blue or anxious feelings. Remember, there is a way out.

Related Advice

Dear June: A few weeks ago, my grandmother died. We were very close and I'm learning to deal with this loss in my own way. The problem I seem to have is people coming to me or calling to ask how I'm doing. I tell them I'm fine and am very cordial. They still just don't seem to understand that I don't need to talk about this every minute of the day. I know they're just concerned and I appreciate them. Would it be wrong to tell them to back off because I don't have the need to nor do I want to talk about it? Please give me some diplomatic advice.

—MC, Hollywood, FL

Dear MC: Apparently, you are coping with this loss; therefore, you shouldn't allow others to stress you out. There is nothing wrong with simply acknowledging their concern and saying you don't want to discuss it. You could add that you will let them know if you need to talk. Definitely be kind. Sometimes we take our pain out on others. Then when we do want them around, our actions may have pushed them away. Don't allow this to happen, and don't keep yourself from dealing with the sadness. Sometimes the best way to cope is to get it all out. Then comes the point to move on. If you've moved on, gently let your friends know that.

• • •

Dear June: Concerning your letter about the mother who hits her daughter. I'll give her credit for admitting it because my mom would never admit how she hurt me. Years ago I went to school in Virginia. From the day my parents dropped me off until two years later when I came home, I had no seizures. After I came home, I began to have seizures again. I have always tried to tell her it was her and dad's stabbing remarks that caused the seizures. Now for the past seven years, I have been in such a deep depression. I need some advice.

—Stabbed daughter, Fort Lauderdale, FL

Dear Stabbed: Once you realized that it was your parents' stabbing remarks affecting your health, it was time for you to move yourself away from them again. If you haven't already, you need to seek counseling for your depression. You should also take good care of yourself. Start by eating healthy, drinking plenty of water and taking walks. Do something positive for yourself—take a class, join a spiritual group, volunteer, etc. Instead of absorbing the negativity from your parents, surround yourself with positive people. Take in that positive energy and learn how to be positive about yourself. Repeat to yourself, "I am the greatest me that will ever be." Believe it and live it!

These suggestions may seem simplistic, but every positive step you take is a step in the right direction. I can't overemphasize, though, the need for you to seek counseling. Contact your local crisis line or Mental Health Association. Depression is a real illness that can be treated. (See the resources at the end of the book for more information and resources on depression.)

• • •

Dear June: Two years ago, my parents got divorced, so we moved to the United States. My brother and I lived with our father, but he had so many problems, all of us moved in with our aunt, uncle and cousin. They are very friendly. After elementary school I went to middle school, and I did a 180-degree turnaround. I had been perfect, intelligent, and quiet. During the summer, I freaked out and realized I was not myself. This did not happen in one day, but over three months. When I returned to school, I realized I'm a new version of an imperfect person. I don't know what to do to help it.

—JOB, Fort Lauderdale, FL

Dear JOB: No one is perfect. People make mistakes. It's human nature to want a break from working hard every day. It's also human nature for a middle schooler, like yourself to "freak out" after the separation of your parents, plus a move to another country. It took over a year for this reality to hit you because you were adjusting to a new life. You moved to a country that was foreign to you and started living with a different family. Then you started school. It takes time to get adjusted to all of this. Once things settled and you had a break in the summer, you probably realized how much things in your life had changed. This is an adjustment for anyone and it's normal for you to have concerns. Instead of taking your frustrations out in school, share your feelings with someone you trust, such as a family member, teacher or school counselor. You realize that something is wrong, which is half the battle. You're already on your way to becoming your old self again. I wish you the best.

• • •

Dear June: I've been trying to find a job for the last few weeks through the classifieds. Someone told me word of mouth is the best resource when job hunting and to tell everyone I know that I'm looking for work. How is telling my neighbor and gas station attendant going to help me find a job?　　　　　—Clueless, Pompano, FL

Dear Clueless: Many employers hire individuals who were referred to them by someone they trust. If you receive a recommendation, there may be a better chance for you to at least get your foot in the door. I worked with a lady once who was in search of a job. She told her landlord. One day he asked her for a résumé and forwarded it to a friend. She was called for an interview, was hired and has been working for the company for several years. Use the classifieds, but don't stop there. Someone you know may have a contact at the company you saw in the classifieds. Remember, you have to go after what you want, not just read about it.

• • •

Dear June: There have been times that you have encouraged people to pursue their goals and dreams. That's a nice suggestion, but is it a realistic one? What about people who have responsibilities such as children, financial obligations, and more? We can't just drop everything to do what we want to do. I think your readers need to understand that you are not talking to us when you encourage others to pursue their dreams.

—Fort Lauderdale, FL

Dear Fort Lauderdale: I'm most certainly talking to you and others who have serious obligations and responsibilities. I never said it would be easy. You first have to know what your goal is and what you need to do to accomplish it. Then formulate a plan to make it a reality rather than a dream. All the while, you have to take care of your responsibility. I will encourage individuals to follow their dreams. Once you give up on your dream, you lose part of your spirit.

The Heart of the Matter

When you're at the end of your rope, you just want to give up and let go. If you hang on, however—and seek help when it's needed—you can get a grip. Then you can pull yourself back up that rope. The struggle is worth the effort, because it's through our struggles that we grow.

I have learned this through my own ups and downs. I have also learned that life is all about these little hills and valleys. It's like a heart monitor: While you're alive, it goes up and down. It's when it stays down that you've got trouble. By learning how to deal effectively with your challenges, you can lessen the down times—the stresses in your life—and improve your health.

Stress causes physical illness, such as high blood pressure. It also causes mental and emotional problems, such as anxiety or depression. In fact, stress affects the entire body, from our hair and skin to our hearts and digestive systems.

Although we can't always control the situations that cause stress, we can control our reactions to them. Here are four steps to help you cope with stress:

STEP 1: DEVELOP A POSITIVE SUPPORT NETWORK

In Chapter 2 we discussed your network of supporters. I would like to elaborate because your PSN is a vital part of helping you hang in there. The most important person in your network, of course, is you. You have to decide that you don't want to be miserable anymore.

Next, develop your spirituality and it will help you progress. Some people pray, some meditate, others do yoga. I don't suggest one over the other, but encourage you to find the spiritual connection that gives you strength. I remember sitting alone crying on the side of my bed one day. I turned from sitting to kneeling and began to pray. It was time for me to make that change.

Then I began to realize that I had a strong support network. For example, my girlfriend, Revella, would come over and say, "Go with me to the store." I would say, "I'm quite happy sitting on my sofa, thank you." She would insist that she wanted company, so I would go. I thought it odd because she always had been quite happy shopping alone. Finally, I confronted her about this, and she told me she was making sure I got out of the house, instead of sitting home feeling blue.

Although I had not told her how down I was, she knew me well enough to know I needed to get out. That's one of the characteristics you should seek out when building your Positive Support Network. I have found that there are several traits you should look for:

Positive Support Network Characteristics:

- Individuals you can trust
- Individuals you can call on day or night
- Individuals who know your needs
- Individuals with positive words

Trust: This is the No. 1 requirement for people in your support network. If you need to talk with someone in confidence about your problem, you don't want them telling everybody else. Trust also means if you need help, you can trust this person to be there for you.

Calling anytime: We all know people who can only be there for us during certain hours of the day, and I do mean day. In other words, don't call after dark. I have the good fortune to have a brother who was and still is there for me regardless of the time. I have called him before dawn while crying, and he would wake up and pray for me. Never once has he complained. Never once has his wife complained.

This does not mean you should wear out your welcome by calling all the time. Have some consideration. You are the first person in your PSN, which means you need to take responsibility for yourself. Try to work out your problem, pray or meditate about it. Only call at awkward times if you feel you are in crisis.

Constant reminding: If loved ones don't know or remember your needs, they cannot be of much comfort to you. The fact that my friend realized I needed to get out of couch-potato mode made the situation easier for both of us. She took care of the problem without being fully aware of what it was—and without offending me. What's the big deal about that? We all know rebellion can kick in when we think someone is trying to tell us what to do. Even when we want their help and know they are right, we go down kicking and screaming. If a friend is able to gently guide you to what's good for you, it lessens the chances that you will put up those walls.

Positive words: If you're already feeling down and out, you certainly don't want someone to add to it by constantly reminding you of your woes. You're trying to get relief from that negative part of your life; therefore, your positive support network should be just that—

positive support. Lean on people who will remind you of the good and bring out the good in you.

Although all the people in your PSN should have these characteristics, they will each meet different needs. For example, my mother is not a very outgoing person, but my best girlfriend is. When I was recovering from my surgery, my mother helped me with my physical needs at home; Revella helped by getting me out of the house.

Of course, this level of trust and caring does not grow overnight. To develop your PSN, first, you must know yourself well enough to know what you need. Then you can let others know how to help you. Next you have to open the lines of communication. Find out what you have in common and how you can meet one another's needs. Remember, having a positive support network is a reciprocal arrangement. Giving is just as important as receiving.

The fill-in-the-blank activity at the end of the chapter will help you know what to look for—and what others will look for in you.

STEP 2: NUTRITION, EXERCISE AND YOUR MENTAL HEALTH

Research has shown that the health of the body has a great bearing on your mental health. Let's face it.

When you have a headache or back ache, your thoughts are not as clear. I'll be the first to tell you that eating right and drinking water were not high on my priority list, but during my illness, I learned a few things that turned my thinking around.

Let's start with water. When we don't drink enough water, we put stress on our internal organs and that makes it difficult for them to function effectively. Without enough water, for instance, our digestive systems cannot efficiently cleanse our bodies of wastes. Our brains, which are about 75 percent water, can become dehydrated, causing headaches and dizziness.

To get water, the best choice is pure water. Juices in moderation are fine, but they are high in sugar and calories. Carbonated drinks contain either sugars or artificial sweeteners and are high in sodium. Caffeinated drinks can make you jumpy. Train yourself to like water. It's readily available, and it really is quite wonderful.

As for food, your common sense tells you what to eat. It sounds like a broken record—plenty of fresh fruits and vegetables, whole grains, lean meats and fish, low-fat dairy products and limited fats—but it's the truth. I have found that cutting down on sugars and processed foods really helps. They give you an instant boost, but soon let you down. If you have trouble with your diet, talk to your doctor or see a dietitian.

A while back, I was encountering a slump after lunch. To remedy this, I started eating a lighter lunch (lean meat or fish and fresh veggies whenever possible). Then I took a 10-minute break for a walk outdoors. It really gave me a boost.

If you can't leave the building, walk up and down the stairs or walk around your desk or do calisthenics. Remember what you used to do in elementary school — touch your toes, touch your waist, touch your shoulders. Put your hands on your waist and twist back and forth. In other words, do some form of exercise. There's a book titled, *Too Busy to Exercise* (Storey Publishing, 1996) that gives you a list of activities you can do at the office.

To sum it up:

- Drink lots of water (eight 8-ounce glasses is recommended).

- During the day, do some form of exercise every two hours—tummy tucks, stretching, calisthenics.

- Take a 10-minute break after lunch and walk outside or around your office.

- At least three times a week, do some form of aerobic exercise that lasts at least 20 minutes. (Have a physical check-up before beginning any exercise program.)

STEP 3: REMEMBER THE CHILD WITHIN

What is it that children do when they fall? They pick themselves up, brush themselves off, start all over again. For some reason, the older we get, the more we forget this childhood lesson. When something goes wrong, we don't want to persevere.

What's so interesting is that we promote perseverance with children and with our friends. Think about this: A little boy strikes out on the baseball field. "That's it," he says. "I'm never going to play ball again."

So, what do you tell him? "That's right. You were terrible. Give up. In fact, I don't think you should play any sports because you're just no good."

NOT! You console, encourage and boost him back up so he will get back on the field. "Nothing beats a failure but a try," I can hear you saying that right now. After a while, the child learns to pick himself up and pull himself back up that rope, even without your verbal reminder.

It's the same with adults. When your coworker is suffering from employee burnout, do you tell her she's lucky to have a job because she has no skills? Of course not, you tell her to do something about it.

Many times employee burnout happens because of low self-esteem. People have a fear of moving to another area because they're familiar with their present job. If you're suffering from employee burnout, it doesn't matter what anyone else tells you, you have to believe in yourself—like a child who is not afraid to try anything.

I often hear people complain that they were overlooked for a promotion or that their boss doesn't appreciate them. My response is, "Since when is it someone else's responsibility to get you where you want to be in your career?"

If you're waiting for someone to lend a helping hand, you could be waiting for the rest of your life. Don't think that there's such a thing as security. People are forced into retirement and let go every day. When you are burned out, it's easier for them to get rid of you because you are no longer doing your best.

If you need a change, ask for it. Your employer may be more willing to help you than you realize. You'll never know unless you ask. Children ask for what they want. You can too.

When you were a child, you learned not to let a fall get you down. Recall that will to keep going. If you are sick or just feel burned out, encourage yourself just as you would a friend.

STEP 4: DO UNTO OTHERS

Sometimes we get so discouraged over our own situations that we forget there are others suffering as well. When I was struggling with my pains and sorrows, my husband got sick. When I focused my energies on him, it distracted me from my situation. When I put myself into my work with my students, I felt better emotionally because I knew I was making a difference.

Our friend Mary used to get so wrapped up in her own problems, that was all she could see. She believed the better things in life came extremely hard for her. One day she was sitting in the dentist's office waiting to be called. A man walked in with his mentally challenged daughter. The daughter followed a ritual of spinning twice before entering a door. Although this must have been frustrating for the father, he was very patient with her. Mary couldn't help but think what a difficult situation that must be. She then looked back on her life. She had gone through some trying times, but she still had use of her faculties, and her daughter is able to care for herself. Mary realized that she is blessed.

Take the time to count your blessings. The next time you start to complain about your job, think about the people who don't have one. The next time you feel pain, think about the people who are paralyzed and can't feel at all. The next time you feel depressed over your lack of skills in any area, think about the people who can't even read or learn a skill.

Get outside of yourself by helping others. Volunteer, share your success stories, think of every-day ways to give of yourself. Finally, think about how you would want to be treated when you're feeling down and remember the Golden Rule. "Do unto others as you would have them do unto you."

Get a Grip Activities

Answer these questions when building your Positive Support Network:

- When I talk to _____, does he/she listen well?

- Does _____ respond positively or negatively?

- Has _____ discussed my situation with others without my permission?

- _____ has a (positive or negative) way of speaking.

- Do _____ and I have a lot in common? (Make a list if necessary.)

- _____'s opposite traits are good for me in what ways?

- I prefer to spend the day with _____.

- Does _____ have children? If so, _____ will be better for me to call at night?

- What's _____'s job like? Would it difficult for me to contact her at work?

- These are my needs in a supportive friend. (Make a list.)

Make a list of the people in your PSN and what needs they can meet for you. And remember, this is a two-way street. You have to be willing to give support back to your friends or you won't have them for long.

DO SOMETHING POSITIVE

Think about how you would want to be treated when you're feeling down. Remember there are others also suffering who may be worse off than you. When you attend to the needs of others, it has a way of making you feel better. Here are ways you can help.

- Your PSN is there for you. Ask the people in your PSN what you can do in return. Better yet, surprise them by doing something special.

- Become aware of the needs of others. Then get out, get active and stop feeling sorry for yourself.

- Learning something new will help occupy your mind and time. This will increase your creativity and make you better appreciate yourself. Then you can share it with others.

- Show your appreciation to anyone who shares their time or talents with you.

"NO MORE PITY PARTIES" PARTY

Gather together a small group of upbeat friends for a Positive Party. Each will bring a covered dish and an affirmation or positive thought. Each will take a turn reading the affirmation and beginning a positive discussion. Eat, drink and be merry while the positive energy flows!

Then you can all truly say in one united voice:

NO MORE PITY PARTIES!

Resources

BOOKS

Ten Days to Self-Esteem
Burns, David, 1993
Quill William Morrow and Co.

Art of Living Single
Broder, M., 1990
Avon Mass Market

Adventures in Singlehood
Shellenberger and Ross, 1996
Zondervan

*You Can't Say That to Me! Stopping the Pain
of Verbal Abuse: An 8-Step Program*
Suzette Haden Elgin, 1995
John Wiley & Sons, Inc.

Positive Addiction
William Glasser, M.D., 1976
Harper & Row

The American Medical Association Family Medical Guide
Random House, New York,

Too Busy to Exercise
Porter Shimer
Storey Communications, 1996

Fit For Life II
Harvey & Marilyn Diamond
Warner Brothers, Inc. 1987

The Holy Bible
King James version

TOLL-FREE HELP LINES

National Association for Self-Esteem
1-800-488-NASE (6273)

National Depressive & Manic-Depressive Assoc.
1-800-826-3632

Domestic Violence Hot Line
1-800-799-SAFE (7233)

Alcohol & Drug Abuse Helpline
1-800-821-4357

Mental Health Association
1-800-433-5959

Special Thanks to ...

my brother, Jeff, for his cartoon creativity and my cousin, Ted, and nephew, Tavares, for their artistic work

my siblings (and their spouses) for all their support

my great friend, Revella, for a list of things too long to name

my editor, Elizabeth Rahe, whose middle name is patient

and giovanni for providing such a lovely poem —

giovanni singleton earned a MFA in Creative Writing and Poetics from The New College of California. Since 1997, she has served as a member of the Board of Directors for Small Press Traffic, a literary arts center in San Francisco. She is the recipient of several fellowships and was most recently selected for the1999 New Langton Bay Area Award for Literature.

Her work has appeared in a number of publications, including "mass ave." (Boston), "no roses review" (Chicago), "Proliferation" (San Francisco) and "The Breast" (Global City Press; New York, 1994). Some of her poems will appear in the upcoming anthology *Beyond The Frontier: African American Poets for the Millennium,* Black Classics Press, Baltimore, MD, edited by E. Ethelbert Miller